YOU PROMPT ME,
O HOLY
Spirit

SECOND EDITION

GLORIA LEE–VOJIN

Scripture quotations taken from the (NASB®) New American Standard Bible®, Copyright © 1960, 1971, 1977, 1995, 2020 by The Lockman Foundation. Used by permission. All rights reserved. lockman.org

ISBN: 978-1-4866-2671-7
eBook ISBN: 978-1-4866-2672-4

Word Alive Press
119 De Baets Street Winnipeg, MB R2J 3R9
www.wordalivepress.ca

WORD ALIVE
—P R E S S—

Cataloguing in Publication information can be obtained from Library and Archives Canada.

Contents

Acknowledgements	v
Foreword	vii
Introduction	ix
I Testify	1
Trusting Father God	2
I Praise Your Name	3
Heal Our Nations	4
Praise to the Father in Heaven	6
Dear Father	8
In Despair	9
Where's God	10
You Prompt Me, O Holy Spirit	11
Call on Jesus's Name	12
A New Year	13
Heaven	14
The Birth of Immanuel	15
Deep Love	16
Mother	18
Heal the Sick	20
Faith of Daniel	21
Father	22
Jesus Emmanuel	23

Behold! I Am Coming Quickly!   24

Our King Is Here   26

Blessings   28

Fear God   30

I Don't Claim   31

The Rescue   32

God's Creation   34

The Race Is Over   35

Let Us Pray   36

About the Author   39

Contents

Acknowledgements	v
Foreword	vii
Introduction	ix
I Testify	1
Trusting Father God	2
I Praise Your Name	3
Heal Our Nations	4
Praise to the Father in Heaven	6
Dear Father	8
In Despair	9
Where's God	10
You Prompt Me, O Holy Spirit	11
Call on Jesus's Name	12
A New Year	13
Heaven	14
The Birth of Immanuel	15
Deep Love	16
Mother	18
Heal the Sick	20
Faith of Daniel	21
Father	22
Jesus Emmanuel	23

Behold! I Am Coming Quickly!   24
Our King Is Here   26
Blessings   28
Fear God   30
I Don't Claim   31
The Rescue   32
God's Creation   34
The Race Is Over   35
Let Us Pray   36
About the Author   39

Foreword

It is my privilege to have the opportunity to highlight the commitment, obedience, and heartfelt love for Jesus exemplified by Gloria Lee-Vojin. As her pastor, and as one of the people who encouraged her to compile her poems into a book, nothing brings me more joy than to see Gloria using her gifts and abilities to exalt the name of Jesus.

You will quickly see Gloria's faith and devotion shining through as you read her poems. These poems express Gloria's love for Jesus as she allows the Holy Spirit to inspire her mind and heart.

Gloria has blessed our congregation with her poems during our worship services, and I know they will bless the reader of *You Prompt Me, O Holy Spirit.* Therefore I would encourage you to read them slowly, reflectively, and allow the profound ideas and convictions expressed in them to wash over you. As you do, I know they will speak to you and deepen your love for the Saviour Gloria follows.

In Christ's service,
Rev. Dr. Keith Sweeting,
First Baptist Church of Owen Sound
October 2024

Acknowledgements

I would like to acknowledge my dear husband Mark for all his great support and encouragement of this project. I would also like to acknowledge my pastor, Rev. Dr. Keith Sweeting, for his encouragement to have my poems published.

Introduction

Dear Readers,

Gloria is a Canadian Christian poet. Upon their retirement, Gloria and her husband Mark moved out to the Grey Bruce area.

After many years of writing, she decided to have her pastor read a few of her poems. He pointed out the gift she had for writing poetry. By the grace of Almighty God and the strong guidance of the Holy Spirit, she was enabled to seek out information on how to go about getting published.

Gloria has titled this book of poems *You Prompt Me, O Holy Spirit*, and appropriately so, as most times she is awakened in the night with the words of a poem, prompted by the Holy Spirit.

"I Testify" was written in the midst of the couple's home renovations. The contractor they had hired bailed on them just before autumn and thus left them in a difficult situation. Many prayers later, our wonderful God provided them with a very diligent contractor.

"The Race Is Over" was written in honour of the death of Gloria's mother. "Behold! I Am Coming Quickly!" was written after Gloria had a vision of the Lord Jesus in which those words were clearly spoken.

Gloria hopes her poems will encourage and bless her readers. She continues to write and, God willing, wishes to publish another book in the near future.

May all the glory and honour be to our Father God in heaven!

I Testify

Father God, I testify of Your great love.
No matter which way the road bends,
I will not let go of You!
Please don't let go of me, Abba God!

I testify of Your greatness,
Of the way You work things out,
For those who love You!
I testify of Your greatness, Abba God!

I testify of Your faithfulness
Even when we cannot see
The end of the tunnel.
Abba God, You see the end and beyond.

I testify of Your mercy and grace,
Of the way You part the waters,
For us to safely have a path through.
I testify of Your mercy and grace, Abba God!

Trusting Father God

Suddenly you get the summons
To walk into the unknown.
Just like Jonah, you think of running away.
Instead trust and obey God on high.
His well will never run dry.

You pray to Father God for courage,
And ask if it's His will
For Him to lead you up this hill.
In obedience, you let Him lead.
By the Father's goodness, you do succeed!

With a grateful heart
You are free, giving glory and honour to God,
Trusting and obeying Father God,
In spite of the fear in your chest.
Turn it over to Him and He will do the rest!

GLORIA LEE–VOJIN

I Praise Your Name

Oh God, You are my Lord!
You sustain me,
For without You
My life would be incomplete.

Your love is unconditional.
Your grace is bountiful.
You washed me
And now I am cleansed!

Teach me to do Your will,
Not let me walk on my own.
Take my hand, dear Father,
To guide me every day.

I praise Your name!
I sing to You!
May this song
Ring out to You!

Heal Our Nations

Oh God, have mercy on us.
Cleanse our hearts and souls.
Guide us on Your path of righteousness.
Lead us to Your Light!

Heal our lands, heal our lands!
Heal our nations, heal our nations!
For this we pray, *amen!*

Every knee shall bow,
To Thee, Lord Jesus.
The rich and the poor
Will come before You!

Heal our lands, heal our lands!
Heal our nations, heal our nations!
For this we pray, *amen!*

We cry out to You, Oh God!
May each and every one yearn to do Your will.
Do not turn Your ears from us,
As we are in despair.

GLORIA LEE–VOJIN

Heal our lands, heal our lands!
Heal our nations, heal our nations!
For this we pray, *amen!*

Praise to the Father in Heaven

Dear gracious Father in heaven,
How glorious is Your name!
Because of Your wonderful grace,
I am given another chance at life.
For here I am writing this letter to You.

Praise Your precious name, O Lord of power and might!
You've given me breath to glorify You.
Your love for me is unconditional.
You chose me to be Your child.
How much more blessed can I be?

May all the world know of the wonderful name of Jesus.
Yes, Jesus,
He who died on that cross because He loves us so much.
He sacrificed His life so that we may be free from our sins.
Believe in Jesus the Son of God.

Why?
So that His precious gift of salvation
and eternal life can be yours.

Choose life.
When our lives on this earth end,
We will be going to one of two places:
Heaven or hell.
What do you choose today?

Holy Father, I pray and hope
that all the people of this world
Will choose to follow Your Son Jesus Christ.
His death on that cross would not have been in vain.
But the victory is His!

As He comes to this earth a second time,
To claim all those who belongs to Him,
Thank You for that wondrous day, Father in heaven!
For then every knee shall bow
and all shall know that Jesus Christ,
Your Son, has won the battle.
The trumpets shall sound.
O what a glorious day it will be!
Praise and honour be to You, our God and Holy Father!
Amen!

Dear Father

Dear Father in heaven,
Can You hear me?
Listen to my cry
As I come before You,
Awaiting Your reply.

You're the Almighty One
Whom we must lift on high.
Your eyes are searching,
Your ears are listening,
For those who are still wandering in the wild.

Father, You come to the rescue of those seeking Your face,
Snatching us up with Your amazing grace!
Your love is unending,
Your mercy ever flowing.
To this we give You thanks and praise!

GLORIA LEE–VOJIN

In Despair

Did you hear Me calling your name
To do thy Father's will?
You just stood up and walked away
As if you didn't care.

I've tried calling one more time.
You walked further and further away.
Please take the time to listen.
You might hear what the Father has to say.

Now I see you coming this way,
Unsure of what to do and say.
Be patient, just listen,
You'll hear our Father's prayer.

Where's God

Where's God? you ask.
In times of crisis.
In times of pandemics.
In times of sickness.
Where's God? you ask.

God's in the same place you left Him!
You took Him out of schools.
You swept Him under the rug.
You live your life like He doesn't exist.
Now you ask, where's God?

God is a fair God.
He lets you have a choice in life.
In your arrogance, you think you can do it all by yourself.
You think you can provide for you.
You think you don't need God around.
Yet you now ask, where's God?

God is loving and forgiving.
Get down on your knees,
Cry out to Him for forgiveness.
Repent and accept Jesus as your Saviour,
And there's God!

GLORIA LEE–VOJIN

You Prompt Me, O Holy Spirit

You prompt me, O Holy Spirit,
On what I should say.
You prompt me, O Holy Spirit,
On how I should pray.

You prompt me, O Holy Spirit,
With writing these words.
You prompt me, O Holy Spirit,
When I cry out to our Lord!

You prompt me, O Holy Spirit,
Every single day!
You prompt me, O Holy Spirit,
How to walk in Your ways.

You prompt me, O Holy Spirit,
I thank You and bless You.
You prompt me, O Holy Spirit,
The friend that I turn to!

Call on Jesus's Name

If you are feeling weary,
If you are feeling burdened,
If you feel like no one cares,
Don't you despair!
Call on Jesus's name!

Call, call, call on His name.
He will make you new
Because He cares for you.
Just call on Jesus's name.
Call, call, call on Jesus's name!

If you are feeling lonely,
If you are feeling sad,
If you feel like you can't take another step,
Jesus will comfort you!
Call on Jesus's name!

Call, call, call on His name.
Know that He loves you.
He's with you every step of the way.
Just call on Jesus's name.
Call, call, call on Jesus's name!

GLORIA LEE–VOJIN

A New Year

O Father in heaven,
A new year You have given.
Your Word, so divine.
Refresh it in our minds,
That they will not unbind.

O Father in heaven,
This is a new year.
Please draw us near.
Renew our hearts,
Our souls impart.

O Father in heaven,
Your gift of a new year.
Refresh our praises.
To You we raise
Our voices in adoration.

Heaven

If I told you
I found a place called heaven,
Would you walk with Me?
No more crying.
No more pain.

If I told you
I found a place called heaven,
Would you be a part of Me?
Flowers blooming.
People laughing.

If I told you
I found a place called heaven,
Would you be My friend?
No more fighting.
Just living as one again.

The Birth of Immanuel

What a day it must've been for young Mary!
Chosen to be the mother of Christ Jesus.
Jesus, brought to this world,
Born as the Messiah, our Saviour.

This little baby boy, born in a manger,
Surrounded by hay and barn animals.
His first cry, in the still of night,
As the brilliant star shone down on Him.

Immanuel, God with us.
A name, chosen long before His birth.
This holy Child and Son of God
Came to the earth for us.

As we celebrate the birth of Christ Jesus,
Let us remember the great love of God!
A love so wonderful,
Our God Immanuel came to be with us!

Deep Love

We all have our crosses to bear
But Jesus Christ carried the heaviest cross of all.
What a sacrifice!
He bore it all for our sins.
Every agonizing breath,
Every nail that pierced His flesh,
All the pain that He endured
Depicted His deep, deep love for us!

When Jesus was sent to this earth,
He knew that on Calvary's cross He would die.
This selfless sacrifice paid for us,
Done to glorify God's will, not His.
As Jesus hung on that cross,
He never thought of Himself
But had love for the thief next to Him,
Promising him eternal life.

Jesus, our Lord and Saviour!
Thanking You, for what You did for us
Could never be enough.

GLORIA LEE–VOJIN

Bless You, Lord Jesus!
Praise Your glorious name!
We humbly come before You, Lord Jesus,
With adoration and love.

Mother

In the beginning, God made a woman.
She was named Eve.
Eve was the first mother on the earth.
Since that time, God has blessed us
with many, many mothers.
This very important role was created
Because God wanted someone who would love, nurture,
and care for His children.

Mothers come in all shapes and sizes.
Some are round, some are short,
Some are skinny, some are tall,
Some are jovial, some are serious,
But all in all, the role of a mother is special!

Mothers wear many hats.
One minute she is a chef, the next she is a nurse,
and she's most often the taxi driver!
She wipes away tears.
She gives big hugs and kisses.
She's a teacher!
Yay! She's cheering from the sidelines
Or she's the best party planner ever!

GLORIA LEE–VOJIN

We thank You, God, for all mothers!
Whether they have already passed on
Or are here with us today,
Thank God for mothers!
Happy Mother's Day to all of our beautiful
mothers in the world!
May God bless you all!

Heal the Sick

I thank You, Son of God,
For placing Your holy hands
Upon the sick,
Healing their bodies
And making them whole again!

Jesus, You made the cripple walk!
You made the blind man see!
You created our bodies.
When they are broken,
Thank You for making them whole again!

I pray, Lord Jesus,
That You heal the sick once more!
According to Your will, Lord Jesus,
They need Your healing touch.
Thank You for making them whole again!

GLORIA LEE–VOJIN

Faith of Daniel

No other gods will I bow down to!
My faith is in Almighty God above.
This is what Daniel said
As he stepped into the lion's den.

The One and only, the One and only,
Precious God up above!

Here we go, me and my friends,
Being thrown into the fiery flames.
Protect us, Father God, we pray!
Be that shield for us once again.

The One and only, the One and only,
Precious God up above!

Our duties we carry out day by day,
But let it be done according to Your will.
Keep us strong as we finish the race.
Father God Almighty, we look to Your face!

The One and only, the One and only,
Precious God up above!

Father

As Christ is the head of every man,
Thus every father ought to be the head of his household.
This is a very significant role that a father has!

Today we honour fathers for their leadership!
We honour them for being providers!
We honour them for their strength!
We honour them for their endurance!
We honour them for their friendship!
We honour them for their skills!
We honour them for their knowledge!
We honour them for setting good examples for their children!

They are not very good at multitasking,
But we can overlook that, as most are good at barbecuing!
They are not too bad at sports either.

We thank God for all of our great dads!
We thank God for our dads who have already passed on
But have left behind a great legacy!
May God bless you and guide you all.

Happy Father's Day!

GLORIA LEE–VOJIN

Jesus Emmanuel

Joseph gathered their belongings
To set out for the city of David.
He placed Mary on the donkey
And began their treacherous journey.

As they reached Bethlehem,
Mary sobbed in pain.
But there was no room at the inn,
Only a lowly cattle shed!

Joseph quickly gathered straw for a bed
In the cattle's drinking trough.
Upon the arrival of the Christ Child,
He would be warm and fed.

Alleluia, Alleluia! sang the host of angels.
Glory to God in the highest!
God lit up the night sky! Our Messiah is here!
The Good News will be spread everywhere!

He shall be called Jesus Emmanuel!
He shall be called Jesus Emmanuel!

Behold! I Am Coming Quickly!

Early one morning, a brilliant blue sky,
Then a cloud, so perfect and shimmering white.
There appeared to me my Lord Jesus Christ!
This humbled child of His.

Jesus says, "Behold! I am coming quickly!"
Alleluia! Alleluia!

My Lord in His dazzling white gown.
His eyes so sad and troubled.
The palms of His hands are uplifted
As He says these words to me.

Jesus says: "Behold! I am coming quickly!"
Alleluia! Alleluia!

This message spoken by Our Lord!
A reminder to the world.
Words of love to all those who will hear them.
A message of hope in times like these.

Jesus says: "Behold! I am coming quickly!"
Alleluia! Alleluia!

GLORIA LEE–VOJIN

Fear not, brothers and sisters in Christ!
Our Saviour keeps His promises.
Be ready for His return!
I believe in what He says.

Jesus says: "Behold! I am coming quickly!"
Alleluia! Alleluia!

Our King Is Here

For God so loved the world,
He sent us His one and only Son!
He came down to this earth,
Born by a virgin birth.
Jesus, our Saviour,
Was laid in a manger!

This holy infant Child,
So meek and so mild,
Was humble when He appeared.
His little heart full of love and care.
He knew His mission before His birth,
Saving His people on the earth.

The shepherds in the field
Were guided by the star.
They travelled from afar.
Instinctively they kneeled
Before this beautiful baby Boy,
Their hearts filled with joy!

GLORIA LEE–VOJIN

Go tell of Your love and kindness!
Spread Your holy Word
To all the nations on the earth
As You command!

Blessings to thy Father!
Blessings to thy Son!
Blessings to thy Holy Spirit!
Three in One.

Fear God

God is my Rock and my Fortress!
Fear God! Fear God! Fear God!
Come in awe before Him
And give Him the glory and the praise!

You are God above all gods!
Fear God! Fear God! Fear God!
In reverence, we come to You,
Praising and glorifying Your name!

Father God! You who are worthy!
Fear God! Fear God! Fear God!
We submit to You, Father,
Out of love and adoration!

In faith and hope we come!
Fear God! Fear God! Fear God!
Thriving to be obedient before You,
As Your children we come!

I Don't Claim

Up to You, I lift my eyes, O God on high!
Mighty and strong is Your love for me.
Whom else should I turn to for shelter?
But You, O God, my shield and protector.

I don't claim to be brave!
I don't claim to be strong!
I don't claim to be unafraid!
But I claim the promises and love of my Lord Jesus!

Raising my hands up to You, Lord,
Giving You the praise and glory!
Cuz without You, Lord, I am nothing.
With strength through Christ Jesus, I take my daily steps.

Never have I felt such love and comfort.
The distress and misery life has to offer
Pales by Your grace and mercy! O God,
Giving me courage and hope to persevere.

The Rescue

What a mess life would be
If I didn't have Jesus Christ living in me!
My Saviour! My Lord!
Help me to live by Your Word.
You rescued this child from the world
By Your great mercy. Thank You, O Lord!

I accepted Jesus Christ into my life
And now I have been crucified with Him.
Take my hand and lead me on
This journey until the race is won!
O Lord, though the roads are rough,
I know You will not forsake me, not even once!

Teach me to be humble every day
As I learn how to live by Your wonderful ways.
May my marching orders come from You only,
So that I can become more like You daily.
Thank You, O Lord Jesus, for Your grace,
For shining Your light on this sinner's face.

ὶ is changing my heart!
ρrand new start!
blessed feeling
ɔre Thee kneeling!
.ι, Father, in the highest heaven!
Amen! Amen! Amen! Amen!

God's Creation

These flowers, so pretty.
The grass is so green.
The treetops reach to the sky.
God created for you and I!

The raindrops drip, drip, drip.
The birds tweet, tweet, tweet.
The bunny hop, hop, hop.
A great big hug from Jesus!

The roar of the lion.
The sheep baa, baa, baa.
The big mud puddle.
Makes me go ha ha ha!

This is God's creation,
For big and for small.
Feel the wind blow, blow, blow
And feel God's great love for all!

GLORIA LEE–VOJIN

The Race Is Over

The race is over.
The time has come
To rest in the arms
Of our loving Saviour!

So peacefully my soul
Soars up to heaven,
Gently drawn by the Father's hand
Up through the beautiful white cloud.

As graceful as the swan glides on,
Or the beautiful sunrise,
So I must leave you now,
Going home to eternity.

Though the tears may flow,
Let it be.
Be glad for me.
I'm now at rest indeed.

Let Us Pray

Oh Father, in the highest heavens!
How glorious is Your holy name!
Bend Your ear to hear my prayer today.
Let us be consumed by You.
Let us be overwhelmed by You.
Let us walk with You.
Let us talk with You.
Let us be led by You.
Let us be taught by You.
Let us love like You.
Let us stand for You.
Let us kneel before You.
Let us be strengthened by You.
Let us glorify You.
Let us praise You.
Let us sing to You.
Let us listen to You.
Let us obey You.
Let us be truthful to You.
Let us be honest with You.
Let us wait for You.
Let us learn from You.

GLORIA LEE–VOJIN

Go tell of Your love and kindness!
Spread Your holy Word
To all the nations on the earth
As You command!

Blessings to thy Father!
Blessings to thy Son!
Blessings to thy Holy Spirit!
Three in One.

Fear God

God is my Rock and my Fortress!
Fear God! Fear God! Fear God!
Come in awe before Him
And give Him the glory and the praise!

You are God above all gods!
Fear God! Fear God! Fear God!
In reverence, we come to You,
Praising and glorifying Your name!

Father God! You who are worthy!
Fear God! Fear God! Fear God!
We submit to You, Father,
Out of love and adoration!

In faith and hope we come!
Fear God! Fear God! Fear God!
Thriving to be obedient before You,
As Your children we come!

I Don't Claim

Up to You, I lift my eyes, O God on high!
Mighty and strong is Your love for me.
Whom else should I turn to for shelter?
But You, O God, my shield and protector.

I don't claim to be brave!
I don't claim to be strong!
I don't claim to be unafraid!
But I claim the promises and love of my Lord Jesus!

Raising my hands up to You, Lord,
Giving You the praise and glory!
Cuz without You, Lord, I am nothing.
With strength through Christ Jesus, I take my daily steps.

Never have I felt such love and comfort.
The distress and misery life has to offer
Pales by Your grace and mercy! O God,
Giving me courage and hope to persevere.

The Rescue

What a mess life would be
If I didn't have Jesus Christ living in me!
My Saviour! My Lord!
Help me to live by Your Word.
You rescued this child from the world
By Your great mercy. Thank You, O Lord!

I accepted Jesus Christ into my life
And now I have been crucified with Him.
Take my hand and lead me on
This journey until the race is won!
O Lord, though the roads are rough,
I know You will not forsake me, not even once!

Teach me to be humble every day
As I learn how to live by Your wonderful ways.
May my marching orders come from You only,
So that I can become more like You daily.
Thank You, O Lord Jesus, for Your grace,
For shining Your light on this sinner's face.

Lord Jesus is changing my heart!
It's a grand new start!
What a blessed feeling
As I pray before Thee kneeling!
Thank You, Father, in the highest heaven!
Amen! Amen! Amen! Amen!

God's Creation

These flowers, so pretty.
The grass is so green.
The treetops reach to the sky.
God created for you and I!

The raindrops drip, drip, drip.
The birds tweet, tweet, tweet.
The bunny hop, hop, hop.
A great big hug from Jesus!

The roar of the lion.
The sheep baa, baa, baa.
The big mud puddle.
Makes me go ha ha ha!

This is God's creation,
For big and for small.
Feel the wind blow, blow, blow
And feel God's great love for all!

GLORIA LEE–VOJIN

The Race Is Over

The race is over.
The time has come
To rest in the arms
Of our loving Saviour!

So peacefully my soul
Soars up to heaven,
Gently drawn by the Father's hand
Up through the beautiful white cloud.

As graceful as the swan glides on,
Or the beautiful sunrise,
So I must leave you now,
Going home to eternity.

Though the tears may flow,
Let it be.
Be glad for me.
I'm now at rest indeed.

Let Us Pray

Oh Father, in the highest heavens!
How glorious is Your holy name!
Bend Your ear to hear my prayer today.
Let us be consumed by You.
Let us be overwhelmed by You.
Let us walk with You.
Let us talk with You.
Let us be led by You.
Let us be taught by You.
Let us love like You.
Let us stand for You.
Let us kneel before You.
Let us be strengthened by You.
Let us glorify You.
Let us praise You.
Let us sing to You.
Let us listen to You.
Let us obey You.
Let us be truthful to You.
Let us be honest with You.
Let us wait for You.
Let us learn from You.

GLORIA LEE–VOJIN

Come, join the celebration
Of this most precious birth!
People of every nation,
Clap your hands and laugh with mirth.
Jesus Messiah, our King is here!
Celebrate, O people everywhere!

Blessings

Blessings to thy Father!
Blessings to thy Son!
Blessings to thy Holy Spirit!
Three in One.

Sing praises to Your name
From deep within our hearts.
It's pleasing to Your ears!
You take us as we are.

Blessings to thy Father!
Blessings to thy Son!
Blessings to thy Holy Spirit!
Three in One.

Come to Your throne
In reverence and humbleness.
Come as a little child,
With a heart full of love.

Blessings to thy Father!
Blessings to thy Son!
Blessings to thy Holy Spirit!
Three in One.

GLORIA LEE–VOJIN

Let us receive You.
Let us repent before You.
Let us be thankful for You.
Let us be loved by You.
Let us pray, let us pray!
Let us pray, in Jesus's name!

About the Author

Gloria Lee-Vojin and her husband Mark live in Grey Bruce, Ontario. They moved to that area upon retiring. She has been writing for many years but has only now decided to get published after being encouraged by both Mark and her pastor.

Gloria's walk with God is strong but has been challenged many times. These challenges have only made her faith stronger in Christ Jesus.

She knows with certainty that without the Holy Spirit prompting her, this book would never have been materialized.

Gloria gives all the glory and honour to our Father God in heaven.

9 781486 626717